This Book Belongs To

_____

_____

CONTENT

 Trace The Lines & Practice

 Trace The Alphabet Letters

 SIGHT WORDS TRACING

 Trace The Numbers & Practice Writing.

 Trace The following shapes.

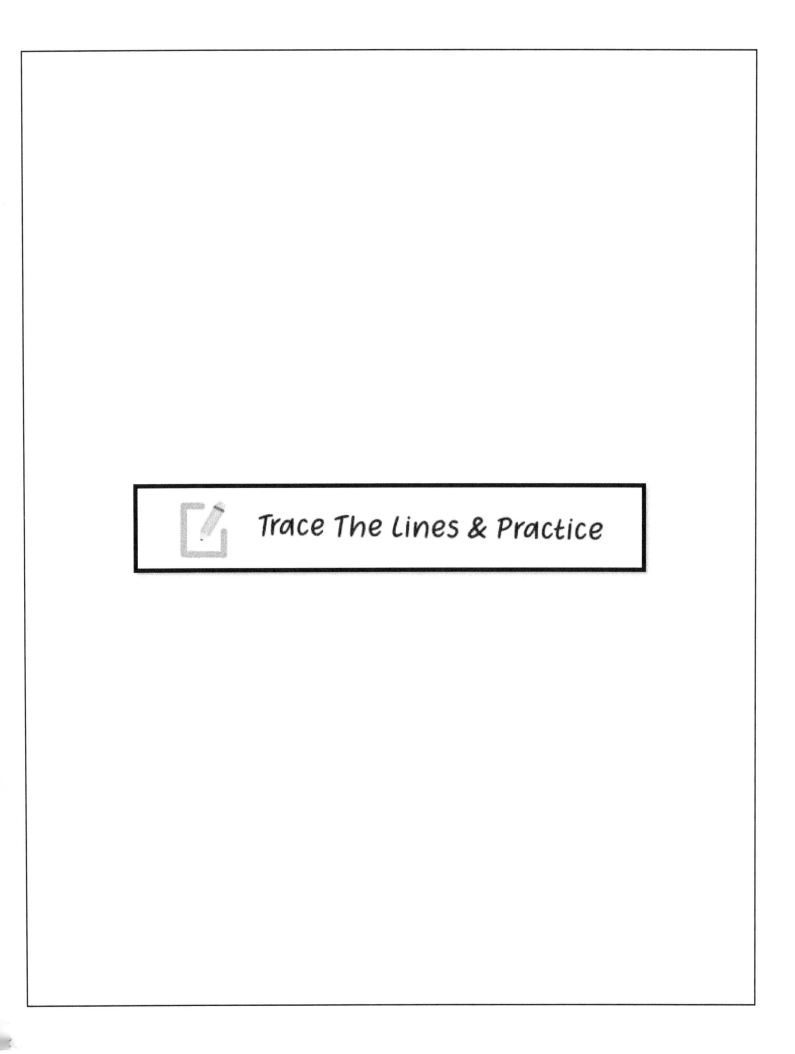

Pen-Control
Lines

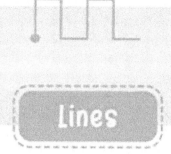

 Trace The Lines & Practice

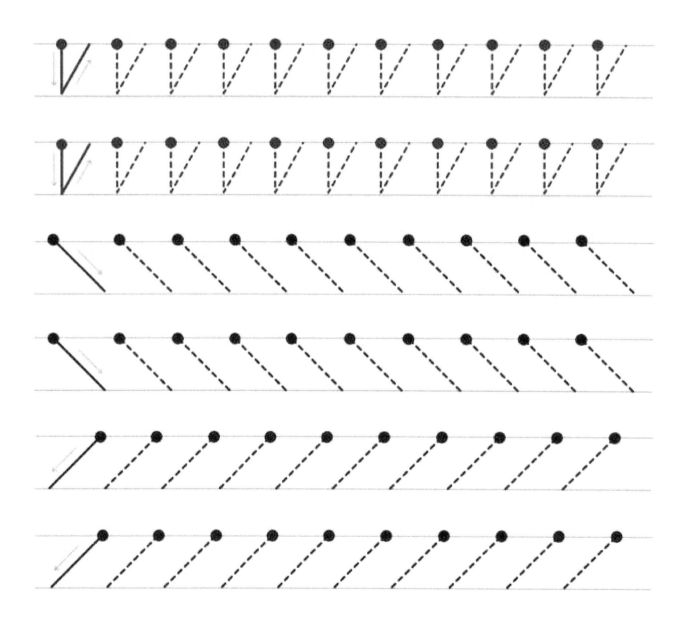

Pen-Control

Lines

 Trace The Lines & Practice

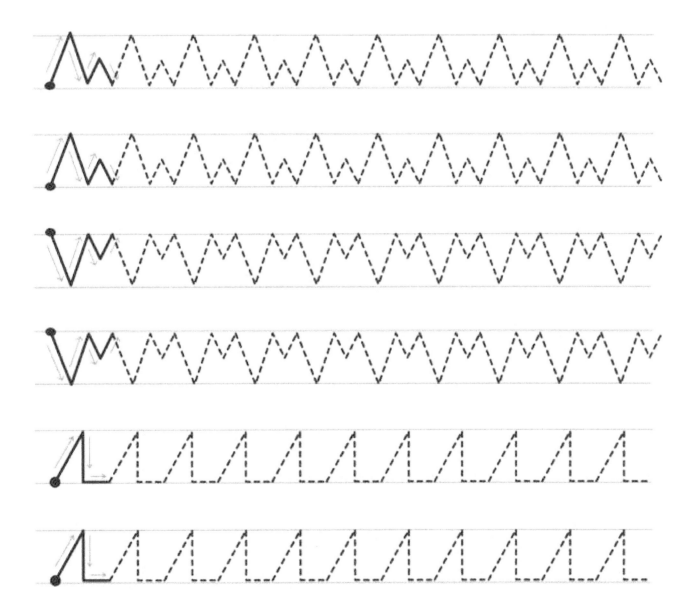

Pen-Control

Curves

 Trace The Lines & Practice

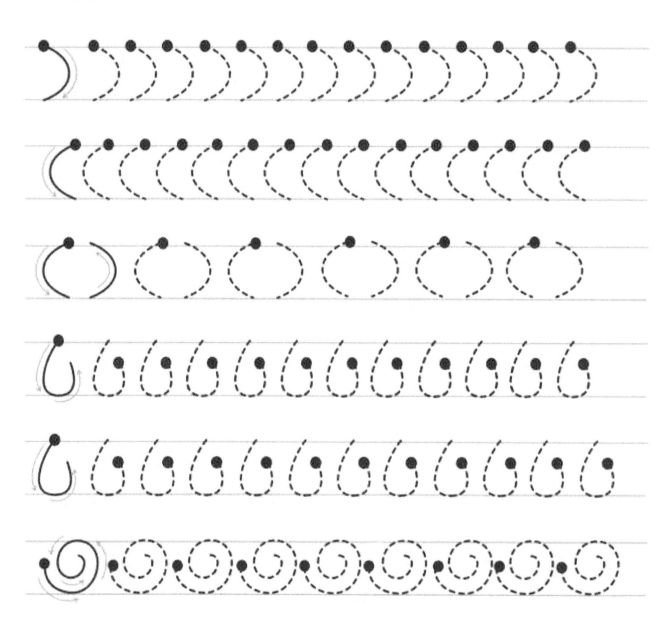

Pen-Control

Lines

📝 Trace The Lines & Practice

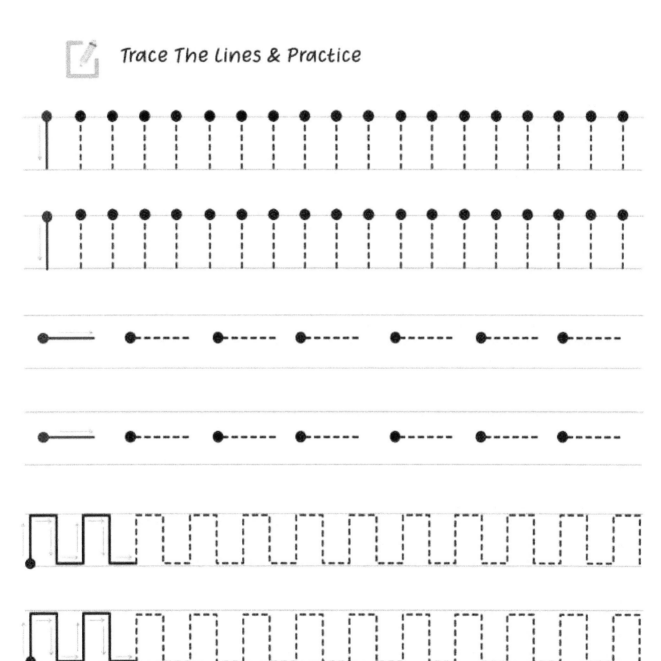

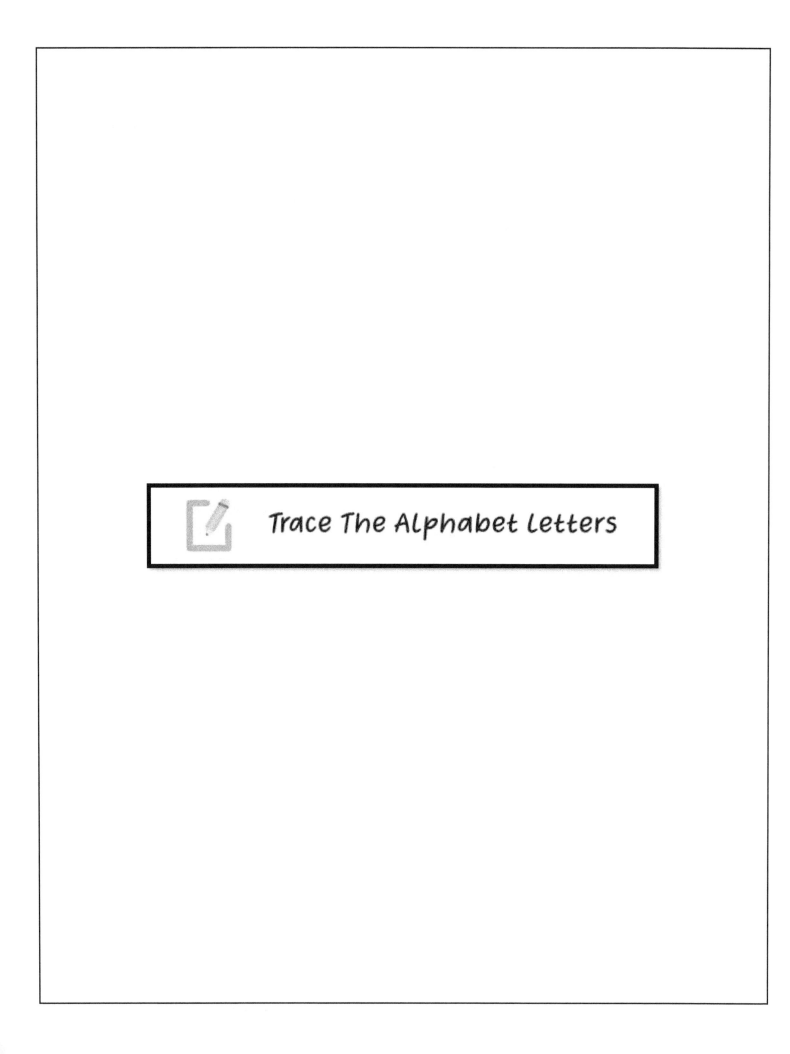

Alphabet

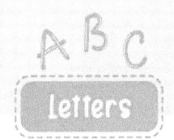

 Trace The Alphabet Letters

A A A A A A
a a a a a a
B B B B B B
b b b b b b
C C C C C C
c c c c c c

Alphabet

Letters

 Trace The Alphabet Letters

D D D D D D D

d d d d d d d

E E E E E E E

e e e e e e e

F F F F F F F

f f f f f f f

Alphabet

 Trace The Alphabet Letters

G G G G G G G

g g g g g g g

H H H H H H H

h h h h h h h

I I I I I I I

i i i i i i i

Alphabet

Letters

 Trace The Alphabet Letters

J J J J J J J

j j j j j j j

K K K K K K K

k k k k k k k

L L L L L L L

l l l l l l l

Alphabet

Letters

 Trace The Alphabet Letters

M M M M M M M

m m m m m m m

N N N N N N N

n n n n n n n

O O O O O O O

o o o o o o o

Alphabet

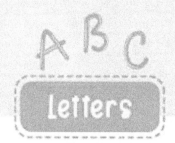

 Trace The Alphabet Letters

P P P P P P
p p p p p p
Q Q Q Q Q Q
q q q q q q
R R R R R R
r r r r r r

Alphabet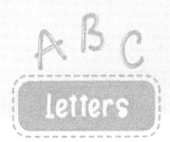

 Trace The Alphabet Letters

S S S S S S S

s s s s s s s

T T T T T T T

t t t t t t t

U U U U U U U

u u u u u u u

Alphabet Letters

 Trace The Alphabet Letters

Alphabet

 Trace The Alphabet Letters

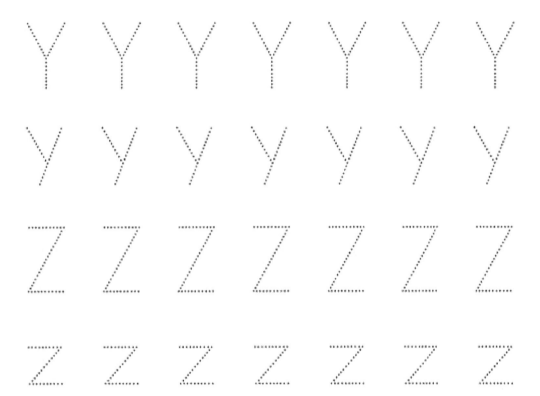

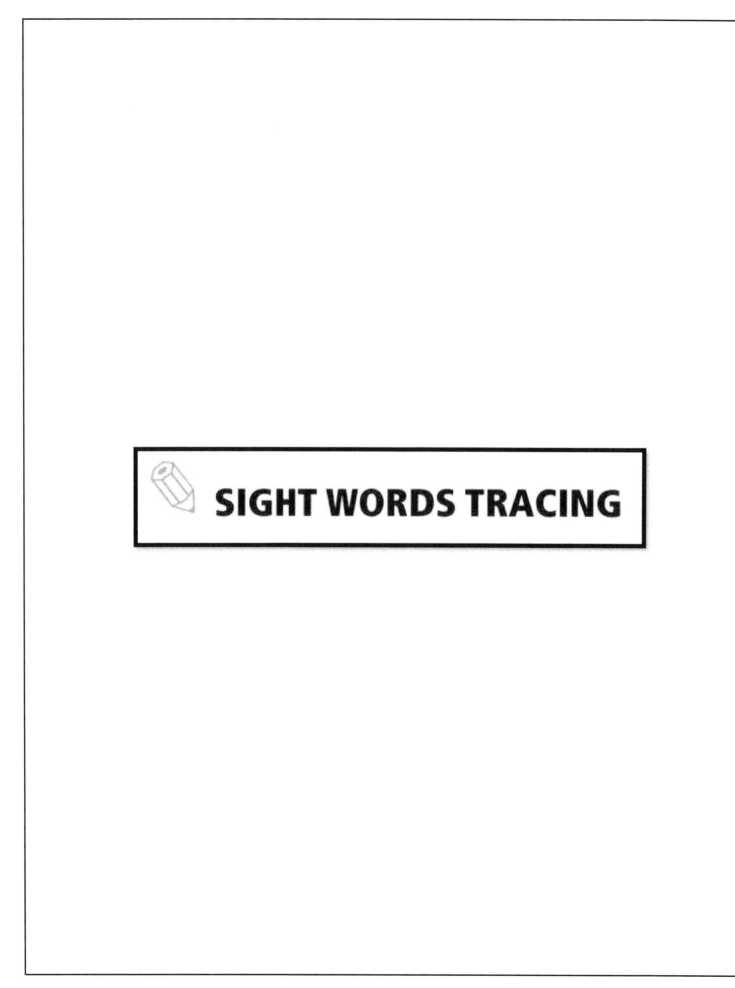

Writing

Trace The Dotted Lines. Then Write Your Own On The Next Line.

Ant Ant Ant

Write The Letter A In The Space Below.

___ n ___ t

Draw a line to match the correct pictures.

- Airplane
- Angel
- Ant
- Apple

All These Words Have The Letter A In Them. Circle The Word Ant.

Apple   Airplane

Axe   Ant

Writing

Word

Trace The Dotted Lines. Then Write Your Own On The Next Line.

Bee Bee Bee

Write The Letter B In The Space Below.

e e

Draw a line to match the correct pictures.

   •   • Bird

   •   • Butterfly

   •   • Balloon

   •   • Banana

All These Words Have The Letter B In Them. Circle The Word Bear.

Ball   **Balloon**   **Bear**

Bus   **Book**

Writing Word

Trace The Dotted Lines. Then Write Your Own On The Next Line.

Cat Cat Cat

Write The Letter C In The Space Below. | Draw a line to match the correct pictures.

__ a t

   •   • Chocolate

   •   • Crab

   •   • Cake

  •   • Cat

All These Words Have The Letter C In Them. Circle The Word Cactus

Carrot   **Cat**   **Cupboard**

Cactus   **Corn**

Writing

A B C
Word

Trace The Dotted Lines. Then Write Your Own On The Next Line.

Dog Dog Dog

Write The Letter D In The Space Below.

___ o g

Draw a line to match the correct pictures.

     •   • Duck

     •   • Drum

     •   • Dog

     •   • Dolphin

All These Words Have The Letter D In Them. Circle The Word Doll

Donut   **Dragonfly**

Doll   **Dinosaur**

Writing  Word

Trace The Dotted Lines. Then Write Your Own On The Next Line.

Egg   Egg   Egg

Write The Letter E In The Space Below. | Draw a Line to match the correct pictures.

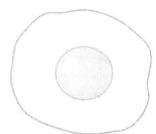

g g

 · · Egg

 · · Eye

 · · Earth

 · · Eraser

All These Words Have The Letter E In Them. Circle The Word Envelope

Envelope   **Earth**

Elephant   **Eye**   **Eagle**

Writing

Word

Trace The Dotted Lines. Then Write Your Own On The Next Line.

Fish Fish Fish

Write The Letter F In The Space Below.

_ i s h

Draw a line to match the correct pictures.

- Fish
- Fork
- Fox
- Flower

All These Words Have The Letter F In Them. Circle The Word Fruits

Flag   **Fly**

Fruits   **Fire engine**

Writing

Trace The Dotted Lines. Then Write Your Own On The Next Line.

Write The Letter G In The Space Below.

__ o a t

Draw a Line to match the correct pictures.

  · Gift

  · Grapes

  · Glasses

  · Gun

All These Words Have The Letter G In Them. Circle The Word Giraffe

Grape **Gingerbread**

Giraffe **Gloves** **Glue**

Writing Word

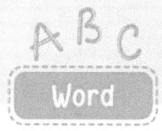

Trace The Dotted Lines. Then Write Your Own On The Next Line.

Hat Hat Hat

Write The Letter H In The Space Below.

_ a t

Draw a line to match the correct pictures.

   • Hedgehog

   • House

   • Hippo

   • Hat

All These Words Have The Letter H In Them. Circle The Word Honey

Hammer   **Honeymelon**

Hippo   Harp   Honey

Writing Word

Trace The Dotted Lines, Then Write Your Own On The Next Line.

Ice   Ice   Ice

Write The Letter I In The Space Below.

___ c e

Draw a line to match the correct pictures.

 · Ice

 · Ice cream

 · Ink

 · Iguana

All These Words Have The Letter I In Them. Circle The Word Island

Insect   **Ice skates**

Iron   **Island**

Writing

Word

Trace The Dotted Lines. Then Write Your Own On The Next Line.

Jet Jet Jet

Write The Letter J In The Space Below.

___ e t

Draw a Line to match the correct pictures.

 • Jellyfish

 • Jar

 • Juice

 • Jam

All These Words Have The Letter J In Them. Circle The Word Jellyfish

Juice   Jelly   Jug

Jellyfish   Jeans

Writing

Word

Trace The Dotted Lines. Then Write Your Own On The Next Line.

Key   Key   Key

Write The Letter K In The Space Below.

_ e y

Draw a line to match the correct pictures.

- Key
- Kangaroo
- Knife
- Kite

All These Words Have The Letter K In Them. Circle The Word King

Knife   **Ketchup**   **Kettle**

Kiwi   **King**

Writing

Trace The Dotted Lines. Then Write Your Own On The Next Line.

Lips Lips Lips Lips

Write The Letter L In The Space Below.

_ i p s

Draw a Line to match the correct pictures.

   • Leg

   • Lemur

   • Ladybug

  • Lamp

All These Words Have The Letter L In Them. Circle The Word Lemon

Lobster   Lion   Lemon

Ladybug   Log

Writing  Word

Trace The Dotted Lines. Then Write Your Own On The Next Line.

Moon Moon

Write The Letter M In The Space Below.

___ o o n

Draw a Line to match the correct pictures.

- Mushroom
- Moon
- Map
- Milk

All These Words Have The Letter M In Them. Circle The Word Mango

Monkey   Mug   Motorcycle

Muffin   Mango

Writing

Word

Trace The Dotted Lines. Then Write Your Own On The Next Line.

Nest Nest

Write The Letter N In The Space Below.

_ e s t

Draw a line to match the correct pictures.

- Neddy
- Nut
- Nest
- Net

All These Words Have The Letter N In Them. Circle The Word Nest

Needle   **Notes**   **Narwhal**

Nest   **Nut**

Writing

A B C Word

Trace The Dotted Lines. Then Write Your Own On The Next Line.

Owl Owl Owl

Write The Letter O In The Space Below.

Draw a line to match the correct pictures.

- Onion
- Orange
- Owl
- Octopus

All These Words Have The Letter O In Them. Circle The Word Orange

Oil   **Orange**   **Octopus**

Onion   **Olives**

Writing

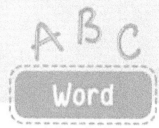
Word

Trace The Dotted Lines. Then Write Your Own On The Next Line.

Panda Panda

Write The Letter P In The Space Below.

_ anda

Draw a line to match the correct pictures.

 •   • Penguin

 •   • Pan

 •   • Pumpkin

 •   • Pen

All These Words Have The Letter P In Them. Circle The Word Pizza

Pizza   **Pillow**

Plate   **Police car**

Writing

Word

Trace The Dotted Lines. Then Write Your Own On The Next Line.

Queen Queen

Write The Letter Q In The Space Below.

_ueen

Draw a Line to match the correct pictures.

 • Quiver

  • Quince

• Quail

  • Quill

All These Words Have The Letter Q In Them. Circle The Word Quill

Quill   Quilt

Quartz   Question

Writing

Word

Trace The Dotted Lines. Then Write Your Own On The Next Line.

Robin Robin

Write The Letter R In The Space Below.

obin

Draw a line to match the correct pictures.

 • • Raccoon

 • • Rain

 • • Rainbow

 • • Rocket

All These Words Have The Letter R In Them. Circle The Word Robot

Radish **Rabbit**

Rug **Robot**

Writing

A B C Word

Trace The Dotted Lines. Then Write Your Own On The Next Line.

Sun Sun Sun

Write The Letter S In The Space Below.

__ u n

Draw a line to match the correct pictures.

 • Snail

 • Snake

 • Soap

 • Socks

All These Words Have The Letter S In Them. Circle The Word Shark

Strawberry   Socks

Shark   Saw   Snowman

Writing

Word

Trace The Dotted Lines. Then Write Your Own On The Next Line.

Tree Tree

Write The Letter T In The Space Below.

__ ree

Draw a line to match the correct pictures.

 • • Turtle

 • • Tomato

 • • Teeth

 • • Truck

All These Words Have The Letter T In Them. Circle The Word Toys

Taxi   **Tea**

Toys   **Train**

Writing Word

Trace The Dotted Lines. Then Write Your Own On The Next Line.

Unicorn

Write The Letter U In The Space Below.

_nicorn

Draw a Line to match the correct pictures.

   Urchin

   Umbrella

   Uguisu

   Uncle

All These Words Have The Letter U In Them. Circle The Word Uniform

Unhappy   Under

Ukulele   Uniform   Unicycle

Writing

Word

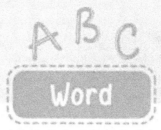

Trace The Dotted Lines. Then Write Your Own On The Next Line.

Vine Vine

Write The Letter V In The Space Below.

_ i n e

Draw a Line to match the correct pictures.

- Violet
- Van
- Vase
- Vulture

All These Words Have The Letter V In Them. Circle The Word Violin

Vegetables   **Vest**

Violin   **Vacuum cleaner**   **Volcano**

Writing

 Word

Trace The Dotted Lines. Then Write Your Own On The Next Line.

Whale Whale

Write The Letter w In The Space Below.

_ h a l e

Draw a line to match the correct pictures.

   •   Watermelon

   •   Worm

   •   Window

   •   Whale

All These Words Have The Letter w In Them. Circle The Word wall

Wall	Watch
Whistle	Wheel

Writing

Word

Trace The Dotted Lines. Then Write Your Own On The Next Line.

X-ray X-ray

Write The Letter X In The Space Below.

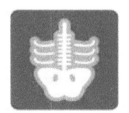

_ - r a y

Draw a line to match the correct pictures.

 • • X-mas tree

 • • Xiphias

 • • Xylophone

 • • X-ray

All These Words Have The Letter X In Them Circle The Word X-ray

Ximenia   **Xylophone**

X-mas   **X-ray**

Writing Word

Trace The Dotted Lines. Then Write Your Own On The Next Line.

Yo-Yo   Yo-Yo   Yo-Yo

Write The Letter Y In The Space Below.

Draw a line to match the correct pictures.

- Yacht
- Yoga
- Yarn
- Yolk

All These Words Have The Letter Y In Them. Circle The Word Yoga

Yogurt   Yam

Yoga

Yak   Yellow

Writing

Word

Trace The Dotted Lines. Then Write Your Own On The Next Line.

Zebra Zebra

Write The Letter Z In The Space Below.

ebra

Draw a Line to match the correct pictures.

 • Zebra

 • Zeppelin

 • Zip

 • Zigzag

All These Words Have The Letter Z In Their Name. Circle The Word Zero

Zodiac   **Zucchini**

Zero   **Zoom**

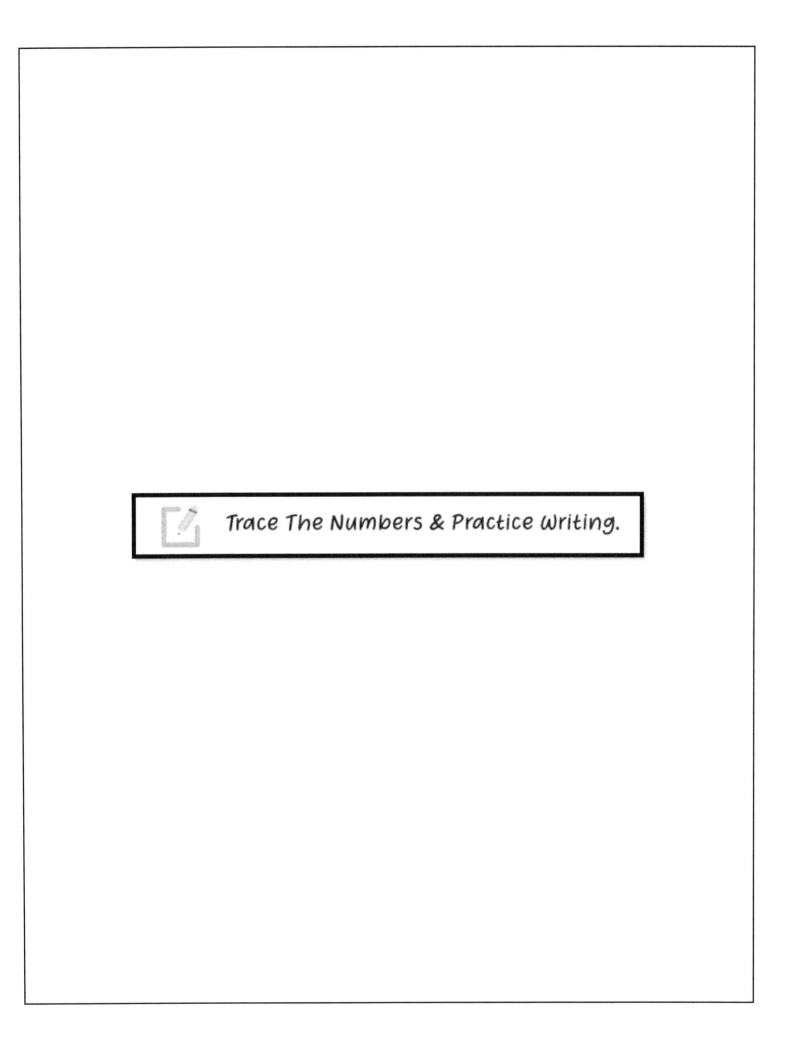

Tracing  Numbers

ONE

GIRAFFE

 Trace The Numbers & Practice Writing.

One One One One
One One One One
One One One One

Tracing

1 2 3 Numbers

TWO

ELEPHANT

✎ Trace The Numbers & Practice Writing.

2 2 2 2 2 2 2 2 2 2
2 2 2 2 2 2 2 2 2 2
2 2 2 2 2 2 2 2 2 2

Two Two Two Two
Two Two Two Two
Two Two Two Two

Tracing Numbers

THREE

TIGER

 Trace The Numbers & Practice Writing.

3 3 3 3 3 3 3 3 3
3 3 3 3 3 3 3 3 3
3 3 3 3 3 3 3 3 3

Three Three Three
Three Three Three
Three Three Three

Tracing Numbers

FOUR

LEOPARD

✏️ Trace The Numbers & Practice Writing.

4 4 4 4 4 4 4 4 4 4

4 4 4 4 4 4 4 4 4 4

4 4 4 4 4 4 4 4 4 4

Four Four Four Four

Four Four Four Four

Four Four Four Four

Tracing Numbers

FIVE

 MONKEY

 Trace The Numbers & Practice Writing.

5 5 5 5 5 5 5 5 5 5
5 5 5 5 5 5 5 5 5 5
5 5 5 5 5 5 5 5 5 5

Five Five Five Five
Five Five Five Five
Five Five Five Five

Tracing 1 2 3 Numbers

SIX

    FROG

 Trace The Numbers & Practice Writing.

6 6 6 6 6 6 6 6 6 6

6 6 6 6 6 6 6 6 6 6

6 6 6 6 6 6 6 6 6 6

Six Six Six Six Six

Six Six Six Six Six

Six Six Six Six Six

Tracing  Numbers

SEVEN

  HEDGEHOG

 Trace The Numbers & Practice Writing.

7 7 7 7 7 7 7 7 7 7
7 7 7 7 7 7 7 7 7 7
7 7 7 7 7 7 7 7 7 7

Seven Seven Seven
Seven Seven Seven
Seven Seven Seven

Tracing Numbers

8

EIGHT

FOX

 Trace The Numbers & Practice Writing.

8 8 8 8 8 8 8 8 8 8
8 8 8 8 8 8 8 8 8 8
8 8 8 8 8 8 8 8 8 8

Eight Eight Eight
Eight Eight Eight
Eight Eight Eight

Tracing 123 Numbers

NINE

OWL

 Trace The Numbers & Practice Writing.

9 9 9 9 9 9 9 9 9 9
9 9 9 9 9 9 9 9 9 9
9 9 9 9 9 9 9 9 9 9

Nine Nine Nine Nine
Nine Nine Nine Nine
Nine Nine Nine Nine

Tracing Numbers

PENGUIN

TEN

✏️ Trace The Numbers & Practice Writing.

10 10 10 10 10 10 10

10 10 10 10 10 10 10

10 10 10 10 10 10 10

Ten Ten Ten Ten Ten

Ten Ten Ten Ten Ten

Ten Ten Ten Ten Ten

Trace The following shapes.

Tracing

Trace the following shapes.

Tracing

Triangle

 Trace The following shapes.

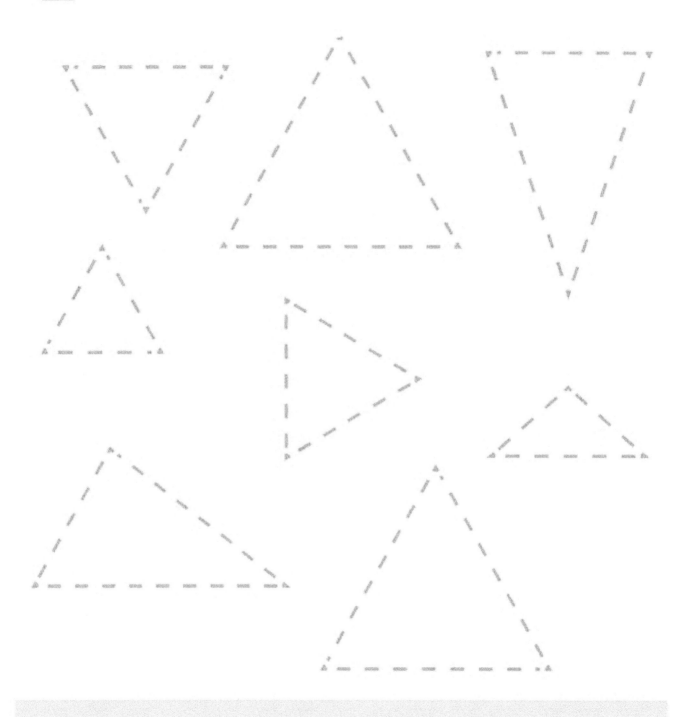

Tracing

Square

Trace The following shapes.

Tracing

Rectangle

Trace the following shapes.

Tracing

Rectangle

✏️ Trace the following shapes.

Tracing

Oval

 Trace the following shapes.

We create our books with love and great care.
Your opinion will help us to improve this book and create new ones.

We love to hear from you.

Please, support us and leave a review!

Thank You!

www.ingramcontent.com/pod-product-compliance
Lightning Source LLC
Chambersburg PA
CBHW061236020325
22805CB00028B/614